The Ravens Selection

Lilly Plum

BookLeaf Publishing

India | USA | UK

Presentation by *BookLeaf Publishing*

Web: www.bookleafpub.com

E-mail: info@bookleafpub.com

ISBN: 9789358314809

First edition 2023

To my Mama. You have always been here for me through the ups and downs and everything in between. You have always encouraged me to step out of my comfort zone and dream big and you have been there for me every single step of the way. Life might not be perfect, but I know I have the perfect mom for this life.

ACKNOWLEDGEMENT

I want to thank anyone in my life who has ever encouraged me, gave me advice, or helped me out in my low moments. I wouldn't be here if it weren't for you. Thank you and I love you.

I would also like to thank my students, who showed me the resilience and kindness that will be the face of our future. Keep being a purple person!

Treasures and toils

In a world where shadows are dark and grey
Ravens gather treasure that breaks the day
These black-winged beauties are wise and free
They find worth in things humans fail to see

Under the moon's silvery beams
Ravens collect shiny things like forgotten
dreams
Coins of forgotten kingdoms, long since passed
Or tales of legacies that didn't last

In the quiet of the night, stars twinkle above
These gatherers continue to search for tokens
beloved
In their ebony beaks is a golden gleam
They carry gems of abandoned dreams

Trinkets and oddities in everything they take
In the raven's realm, there is nothing they
forsake
Their nest, a trove of hidden wonders and
delight
An endless treasure hidden from the light

When you see a raven in the sky
See what it collects, and if you think, you'll
know why
These feathered poets, with trinkets in tow,
Reminds us that beauty is everywhere we go

Diego the Diablo

To my crazy, fluffy feline friend so dear
You always fill me with lots of cheer
You pounce on moths with grace
Chasing them all over the place

You have whiskers and eyes so fair
And such a big belly beyond compare
He has six orange toes on one mitten
When I look at him, I am smitten

He plays with balls
And run into walls
He chases springs
And that's his thing

His energy will never cease
Even when I wish for peace
But you look so fine
I'm so happy you are mine

You have such a kissable face
I want to give you a big embrace!
Even when you leave a big mess
I still love you, I must confess

A para-dream

Wherever you need me, I'll be at your side
That is this young para's greatest pride
Whatever emotion you feel, have no fear
I will always lend you my listening ear

With each new day, I see your brilliant minds
grow
Basking in that promising glow
Life may sometimes feel like a winding maze
But I'm filled with hope when I see purpose in
your gaze

We've shared it all, from lessons to laughter
Every day is a bright new chapter
With all your knowledge and kindness, each day
I find
A future that will be compassionate, fair, and
kind

Bass Gas

5

There once was a bass
Who had a lot of gas
He knew he couldn't stay
He needed to swim away
Oops! Too late! The bass's gas has passed.

Whispers of the forest

In the beating heart of the forest's green embrace
Lady nature weaves her tranquil grace
There are ancient oaks; their stories untold
And the quiet creek with secrets old

Beneath her canopy, on the forest floor
Lies a breathtaking world through a hidden door
There, the mushrooms dance
And the little animals prance

The birds in the treetops sway,
Composing melodious ballads for the day
The rhythm of life where secrets are told
Generations of stories she will hold

In the beating heart of the forest green embrace
Your spirit will wander, your soul will find its
place
Listen to the song of the trees
And you will find a place where your mind is at
ease

When you enter her woods so grand
Take the forest's outstretched hand
Her whispers hold the answers you seek
The heart of nature, where dreams do speak

Flowers

Luscious greens and deep blues
Oh how I love you
The dew on your leaves
Is as sweet as can be
With petals of the brightest hue
Very few
Can make my life
As bright as
You

Benny's Snack Adventure

8

There once was an Otter named Benny
He needed lots of snacks for his belly
He bought some frogs and clams
It got crowded, so he decided to scram
Now Benny's tummy is no longer empty

Memoirs of a moonlit heart

I'm from moon-lit nights and starry skies,
From bonfires and sleepless nights.
I'm from endless summer nights to movie
marathon delights.
I'm from a house not filled with riches but filled
with the richest of love.
I'm from fictional characters that I'm way too
attached to and books upon books
In neatly organized rows.
I'm from my mother, who works harder than
most and shows me what it means to be selfless
and loved.
I'm from my father, who always ensures I have
what I need to succeed.
And I'm from my brother, whose gentle nature
leads and persistence in the face of adversity
Leaves me feeling awestruck and proud
I am from myself.
I know where I come from
But I don't know where I'll go.
So I'll keep these memories in mind
And hope I find
The right path as I go.

Beyond Blood

The dictionary defines family as the descendants of a common ancestor, a shared blood. But that's not how I define family. I do not define it as shared DNA or genes, nor do I define it as a group of people who live under the same roof. No, it's much more vast and complicated than that.

I define family not by blood but by the heart you give and the love you receive. And as scary as that might be, wearing your heart on your sleeve will show how deep your love for others is and will allow them to see where their real family lies.

Family is the bond forged through dawn's delight and night's darkest hour. Family wipes away each tear that falls from your eye and each laugh that leaves you breathless with delight. The people you call family prove to you that you'll never be alone and provide a steady presence full of love, support, and understanding.

Family is the friend turned confidant, the mentor who guides and uplifts; it's your fury companion who wags their tail in delight. Sometimes family can be the stranger that lends a helping hand or a person or place that feels like home wherever you go.

Family is a constellation of lost souls found together on this ship called life. When life throws you to the sea, your family is a hidden lifejacket that can sometimes be hard to see. Family is a complicated web full of love and mistakes; it's full of homecomings and heartbreak. You and your family are a work of art, a grand masterpiece thousands of years in the making. So share with them life's triumphs and failures, your hopes and disasters. Always remember, family is not a definition but a feeling. Choose your family, and don't be afraid to let it grow that way you will never be truly alone.

Icarus's Flight

Sometimes I wonder how Icuras felt
As he was falling to his death.
Did he know he was meeting his fate?
Did he fall joyfully to the heaven's sweet
calling?
He reached for the sun with wings of wax and
dreams
Wanting to touch its golden beams

Upon that euphoric feeling
His wings did fail
How brief that taste of freedom
That still lingered on his tongue

And when his wings of wax and dream did fail
The sun he touched turned into an endless night
Nevermore to feel hope's great delight

Trying desperately to defy his earthly ties
But flying too high, he met his fate
Falling into a watery grave

His once great wings of wax and dreams
Turned to ordinary feathers
Surrounding his body in a halo of endless white

Icarus's cautionary tale is one of hope and pride
So remember this:
With every dream, there's a limit to our might.
A lesson in humility and hubris, a balance to
remind us of what is right.

Sunset's Promise

I'll never forget the sunset that ends the day's despair
As it sinks quietly into the night's gentle air.

The days are filled with toils and troubles, it's true
And the nights I lose myself in the growing chill
But still, I can never forget the sunset.

As the sun sinks gently to say goodnight
I bathe in its rays of dying light
And in its fading embers is where I find my rest
This is a gentle reminder of all that's left

In the times I falter and surrender to darkness and regret
The warm glow of sunset, I'll never forget
It will be a beacon through the night
A symbol of hopeful light

The life of an average writer

Writing is my therapy. When I write I am unstoppable. The galaxy is my stage and I am its creator. With every stroke of my pen or tap of my keyboard, I become the master of life and death itself. In every inhale I have the power to breathe life into the inanimate, and with every exhale I can raze cities to the ground. My imagination knows no limits, my power has no bounds.

Every word I make fills me with endless power. With each brilliant word, I become a God of my own universe, shaping destinies or destroying lives, finding true love or life spent alone. I hold the key to the universe, I am the holy grail.

As I craft each story the world is mine. I am not confined by gravity or time. Minutes slip by with each careful word. The world goes by in a colorful blur. In each story I make, I leave a little piece of me, hoping and praying my reader finds purpose in my words.

I am an artist of my own design. I paint with the colors of hope and tragedy, love and fear.

Whatever I create, I leave a piece of me hoping beyond all that my words will touch and inspire, making my journey as a writer all the more worthwhile.

So if you want to write, then write. There is no right or wrong, good or bad. Create and create from the heart. Life and death is yours for the taking. Being a writer is more than putting words on a page or worrying if you did a good job. Writing is about YOU.

Pour every single thought and dream into this canvas of creation. In your writing, you learn the depth of your mind and how far your imagination stretches. Writing is my sanctuary, and I hope to share it with you. Write for you and no one else and in doing so you may inspire others on the journey too.

Eternal Starlight

I like to think that when I die, I'll become a star
I'll shine down on those I love from afar
No longer will I be bound to earth; my soul will
be free
I'll sing and dance to a song of hope and peace
for all of eternity

I'll watch over those I love, a gentle guardian
shining bright
Guiding you across the dangerous night
I'll be in the constellations, a timeless story in
the sky
No matter how far apart we are, I will love you,
so please don't cry

Although my body will rest quietly in the earth,
my essence will remain
Don't fret; I'll be a glistening star in the infinity
of space, forever free from pain
I will hold our memories and be a symbol of a
love so strong
Here, in this celestial tapestry, is where I truly
belong

When you look longingly into the night
Remember that I am with you, forever in your sight
I like to think that when I die, I'll become a star
An infinite reminder of all that we are.

Shadows

In the shadow of your love, I'll stand
Always yearning for your distant hand
"You're not doing enough!" you say
So I'll hide myself away

Nothing I do is ever right
You make me measure my worth each night
You insult most things I like
Then you wonder why we fight

And in the morning light, I'll try again
Always wishing you would let my love win
But in the end, I hope you'll see
I am enough because I am meant to be.

Glass Child

I'm a glass child
With a temper, oh, so mild.
Content to smile
And to never be wild
I'll set aside my pride
And divide my time
to help you provide.
Am I invisible?
I really can't say
But it sure feels like
It anyway.

Beneath the mask

"You remind me of a ray of sunshine!"
Life is a storm and I know what it feels like to
be without a light.

"You always know how to cheer everyone up!"
I can't let you leave without letting you know
how important you are.

"I love how empathetic and kind you are."
I know about struggling. I have tasted the
hardships of life.

"You are the kindest person I have ever met!"
I'm kind because I have to be. I have gone
without kindness, and the wound runs deep.

"You are so selfless!"
I want to know if I mean something to someone.
Everything I do, I do for others. I exist to serve,
but never be served.

Screaming in silence

I told you I was struggling too.
You said, "Your brother struggles harder than
you."
Fuck you.
Fuck you.
Fuck you.
I was a kid.
I lost my voice, screaming for help.
Begging,
Pleading,
Hoping
That someone, anyone, would hear me.

Dreamer to survivor

There's a little girl with her head in the sky
And a million stars that twinkle in her eyes
She lives in a world of her own
Always dancing with her eyes closed and all
alone

She has moondust in her veins
And a thousand stories inside her brain
This girl lives in her dreams
No one notices that not all is as it seems

She wraps herself in a mask of sunshine
Wishing they would see that she wasn't fine
No one cares, she thinks, so she makes plans to
go away
When in reality she hopes someone will beg her
to stay

This little girl, she is older now
She's made it this far, though she doesn't know
how
Her emotions are a mess of contradictions
And her head is full of hopeful predictions

This not-so-little little girl is finally taking her
stand
She's learning how to accept an offering hand
A lot of days are still filled with clouds
But she really hopes that she made that little girl
proud

Weighted whispers

Being a fat girl is fine until it's not fine. It's fine
when the foreign tiktoker visits America and
makes fun of the plus-size mannequins. It's fine
when the fat girl goes to the doctor for a broken
arm and the doctor focuses on her weight and
not her pain. It's fine when the fat girl finally
works up the courage to go shopping with her
friends, and she stands on the sidelines too
scared to even look at the clothes she knows will
never fit her. It's fine that she was excited to go
into a store that offers plus-size clothing, but the
biggest size they offer is a large. It's fine when
you need to talk politics and start sprouting that
"every body is beautiful" bullshit when the
second you're out of the limelight, you make a
fat joke. A fat girl is only fine when you need to
make a joke or make someone else look better.

Being a fat girl is fine until it's not fine.

It's not fine when that fat girl is wearing
something that makes her finally feel beautiful,
and then the person she's with makes an
unthinking fat remark. It's not fine when that fat
girl is thirteen years old and decides she needs to

starve herself to fit into a world with oppressive and unrealistic beauty standards. It's not fine when the clock says 3 a.m. and the fat girl lies in her bed, silent tears tracing paths down her cheeks as she claws at her own body, as though trying to escape her own skin. It's not fine when the fat girl is left alone in the dark with the echoes of the day's cruel remarks causing a tornado of self-hatred to spin around her head. It's not fine when the fat girl traces her body with her fingers, making plans on where she would take the scissors to eliminate the most flaws.

Being a fat girl is fine until it's not fine. The struggle is real, the scars are invisible, and the battle is endless.

Little Moments

Sometimes I stop and take in the view
I look around the changing world and find
something new
Chaos and strife are always present
So I try to search for something pleasant

Amid the chaos and strife, I seek a clue
To find a bit of hope in the skies so blue
I'll take a rest in the quiet of the moment
As I sit to make an atonement

I look at the little things around me
Noticing the insignificant joys that set my spirit
free
A random smile, a child's joyful play
A million sounds that remind me to savor the
day

Life has no guarantees; that much is true
But look for a silver lining and you'll make it
through
So in this ever-changing world, with all its
complexities,
I'll embrace life's mysteries and find
serendipities.

A Tightrope of Love and Hate

I hate you. I hate you because, when I really needed you, you were never there. I hate you because you treat us like shit, and you sit on your ass all day telling us what to do. I hate you because you would never bother to show up to my performances. I hate you because I have no idea what love is supposed to look like. I have no grand example of timeless love, and I am completely and utterly terrified of marriage. I hate you because you can never be wrong and God forbid someone calls you out on your mistakes. I hate you.

I love you too. I love you because you are in all of my childhood memories. I love you because when it was just the two of us with a fishing pole on the lake, it was calm, and I was content. I love you because you have taught me so much. I love you because I know that strictness and overprotectiveness come from a place of love. I love you because I know you love me. I love you even when we argue. I love you even when my brain tells me to stop. I love you even when I want to hate you.

www.ingramcontent.com/pod-product-compliance
Lightning Source LLC
LaVergne TN
LVHW021333200726
843509LV00014B/2524